SANJEEV KAPOOR

DAL AND KADHI

Published by
POPULAR PRAKASHAN PVT. LTD.
301, Mahalaxmi Chambers
22, Bhulabhai Desai Road
Mumbai - 400 026
for Khana Khazana Publications Pvt. Ltd.

First Published 2008
Second Reprint 2014

(4163)
ISBN – 978-81-7991-415-1

Design: Quadrant Infotech (India) Pvt. Ltd
Photography: Bharat Bhirangi

PRINTED IN INDIA
by Infinity Advertising Services Pvt. Ltd.
D – 4/2, Okhla Industrial Area Phase-1
New Delhi 110020

SANJEEV KAPOOR

DAL AND KADHI

In association with Alyona Kapoor

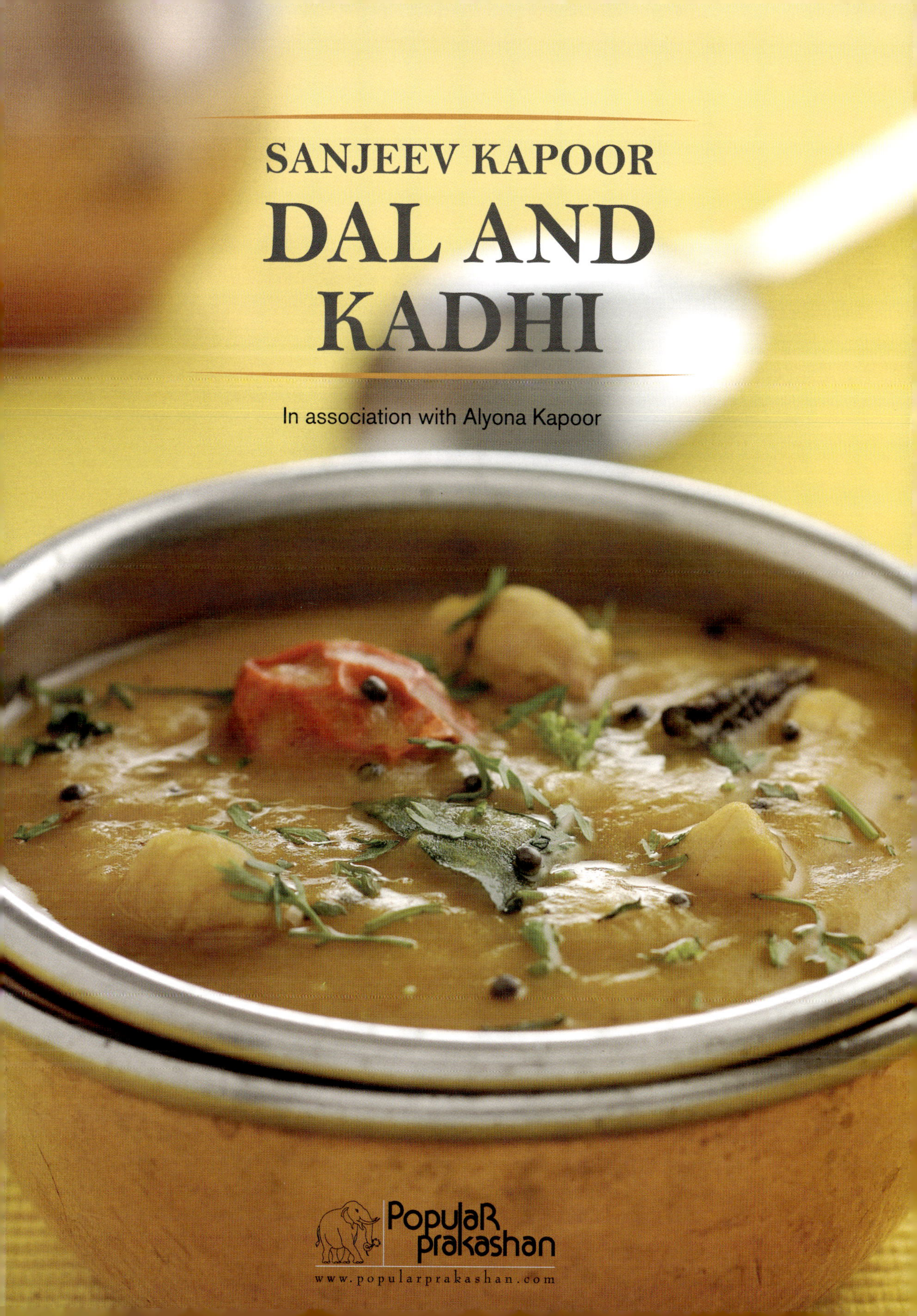

Popular Prakashan
www.popularprakashan.com

AUTHOR'S NOTE

Whenever I am asked what my favourite dish is, I often answer 'Punjabi Kadhi'. My love for *kadhis* and *dals* can be judged by the fact that I never eat just one *katori* of *dal* or *kadhi*, it has to be at least two or more. Which reminds me of the time I was in Wellington, New Zealand and my friend Anu Mehra got upset with me because I skipped a meal cooked by her. She was upset because she was left with too much *dal* (which I would have otherwise eaten)!

As I grew up and learnt more about the many cuisines of the Indian subcontinent, I was amazed by the variety of *dals* and *kadhis* cooked in Indian households.

My exploration further aided my understanding about the deep and intense connection of *dals* and *kadhis* with regional cultures and practices. The rich culture of a region reflected in the authentic, subtle yet intense flavours of the food, have left an indelible mark on my memory.

I often take unadulterated pleasure in making and eating *dals* and *kadhis*: it can be after a hectic day or it can be while hosting a party for friends! It is a fact that *dals* and *kadhis* are comfort foods and they are a good source of calcium, phosphorus, vitamin B and iron. *Dals* are a major source of dietary fibre and protein. *Kadhis* which are a blend of yogurt and herbs assist in efficient digestion. Every region has its locally grown herbs and spices which are used as the key ingredients and as a result, a variety of *kadhis* are relished across the length and breadth of India.

AUTHOR'S NOTE

With this book *Dal and Kadhi* I wish to share my collection of recipes – some of which are household names such as *Dal Makhni*, *Sambhar* and *Ganthia ni Kadhi* along with many traditional recipes, such as *Masaledar Rangoon Vaal*, *Dal Lucknowi*, *Rajasthani Panchmel Dal* and *Maharashtrian Kadhi* that portray the diverse Indian cultural heritage.

All recipes serve four people keeping in mind there are other complementary dishes in the meal.

I am sure you will enjoy reading and trying out the assorted flavours of the various *dals* and *kadhis*. Steamed rice and hot *chapatis*... this way, please!

Happy Cooking!

ACKNOWLEDGEMENTS

Afsheen Panjwani

Anupa Das

Ashwini Patwardhan

Bharati Anand

Bhartendu Sharma

Harpal Singh Sokhi

Jyotsna & Mayur Dvivedi

Mrs. Lata Lohana & Capt. K. K. Lohana

Namrata & Sanjiv Bahl

Neena Murdeshwar

Puja & Rajeev Kapoor

Rajeev Matta

Rita D'Souza

Sanjay Thorat

Saurabh Mishra

Shilpa Rane

Smeeta Bhatkal

Tripta Bhagattjee

Vinayak Gawande

CONTENTS

CONTENTS

AAMRAS KI KADHI

The King of Fruits in a scintillating curry! Must make it every mango season... if you want to leave out the green mango, increase the amount of buttermilk and ensure that it is sour.

Ingredients

1 cup unripe green mango pulp

1 cup ripe mango pulp

3 tablespoons gram flour (*besan*)

Salt to taste

1 cup buttermilk

1 tablespoon oil

A pinch of asafoetida (*hing*)

½ teaspoon mustard seeds

¼ teaspoon fenugreek seeds (*methi dana*)

6–8 curry leaves

2 green chillies, slit

½ cup *boondi*

Method

1. Mix together the unripe and ripe mango pulp, the *besan* and salt till smooth. Stir in the buttermilk.
2. Heat the oil in a deep pan; add the asafoetida, mustard seeds and fenugreek seeds and sauté till the mustard seeds begin to splutter. Add the curry leaves and green chillies and sauté for two minutes.
3. Stir in the mango mixture. Add a little water if required and bring to a boil. Lower the heat and simmer for ten to fifteen minutes. Add approximately two cups of water to get the desired consistency.
4. Add the *boondi* and simmer for five more minutes. Serve hot.

DAL LUCKNOWI

This dal takes on a smoother, fuller texture as it contains milk... an ingredient which will come as a surprise to many.

Ingredients

1 cup split pigeon peas (*toovar/arhar dal*), soaked
2 green chillies, chopped
½ teaspoon turmeric powder
Salt to taste
2 tablespoons oil
1 teaspoon cumin seeds
4 dried red chillies, broken into large bits
5 garlic cloves, chopped
A pinch of asafoetida (*hing*)
1 cup milk
2 tablespoons chopped fresh coriander leaves

Method

1. Pressure-cook the *dal* and green chillies with two cups of water till the pressure is released twice (two whistles). Remove the lid when the pressure has completely reduced. Add the turmeric powder and salt and bring to a boil; lower heat and continue to cook.
2. Heat the oil in a small pan; add the cumin seeds, red chillies, garlic and asafoetida and sauté till fragrant. Pour the sizzling spices into the simmering *dal* and mix well. Stir in the milk and one cup of water and continue to simmer for two or three minutes.
3. Adjust salt, garnish with coriander leaves and serve hot.

BAINGAN KI KADHI

The addition of methi pakoras is a real delight and makes this recipe fit for a party... place a huge platter of fluffy basmati rice alongside.

Ingredients

10–12 baby brinjals (*baingan*), halved
1½ cups yogurt
¾ cup gram flour (*besan*)
Salt to taste
½ teaspoon turmeric powder
1 teaspoon red chilli powder
1½ tablespoons ginger-garlic paste
2 medium bunches (600 grams) fenugreek leaves (*methi*), chopped
2 medium onions, chopped
1 tablespoon oil + for deep-frying
¼ teaspoon fennel seeds (*saunf*)
¼ teaspoon mustard seeds
1 teaspoon cumin seeds
¼ teaspoon fenugreek seeds (*methi dana*)
¼ teaspoon onion seeds (*kalonji*)
4 dried red chillies, broken into large bits
5–6 curry leaves
1 tablespoon chopped fresh coriander leaves

Method

1. In a bowl, mix together the yogurt, two tablespoons of *besan*, salt, the turmeric powder, chilli powder, half the ginger-garlic paste and two cups of water.
2. In a separate bowl, mix together the *methi*, remaining ginger-garlic paste, the onions, remaining *besan* and salt.
3. Heat the oil in a *kadai*; drop small portions of the *methi* mixture into the hot oil and deep-fry till golden. Drain the *pakore* on absorbent paper.
4. Deep-fry the *baingan* in the same oil. Drain on absorbent paper.
5. Heat one tablespoon of oil in a pan; add the fennel seeds, mustard seeds, cumin seeds, fenugreek seeds and onion seeds. When the seeds begin to splutter, add the red chillies and curry leaves.
6. Stir in the yogurt mixture and cook, stirring continuously, till the *kadhi* thickens. Add the *methi pakore* and fried *baingan* and bring the *kadhi* to a boil. Garnish with coriander leaves and serve hot.

EK THALI DAL

Dal with a rich twist as cashew nuts and poppy seeds add a nutty flavour. The inclusion of leafy vegetables makes it more nutritious.

Ingredients

1½ tablespoons split red lentils (*masoor dal*), soaked

1½ tablespoons split Bengal gram (*chana dal*), soaked

1½ tablespoons split green gram (*dhuli moong dal*), soaked

2 tablespoons chickpeas (*kabuli chana*), soaked overnight

¼ teaspoon turmeric powder

½ teaspoon red chilli powder

1 medium tomato, chopped

Salt to taste

1½ tablespoons oil

1 small bunch (150 grams) fresh spinach leaves (*palak*), chopped

1 small cabbage, chopped

2 teaspoons ginger-garlic paste

2 teaspoons grated jaggery

1½ tablespoons lemon juice

Masala

1½ teaspoons poppy seeds (*khuskhus*)

8–10 cashew nuts, chopped

2 dried red chillies, broken into large bits

1 teaspoon coriander seeds

2 cloves

1½ tablespoons grated fresh coconut

Method

1. For the masala, soak the poppy seeds and cashew nuts in one cup of water for thirty minutes. Drain and grind to a fine paste with the red chillies, coriander seeds, cloves and coconut.
2. Pressure-cook the *dals* and *kabuli chana* with three and a half cups of water, the turmeric powder, chilli powder, tomato and salt till the pressure is released four or five times (four or five whistles), or till soft.
3. Heat the oil in a *kadai*; add the spinach and cabbage and sauté for about five minutes.
4. Add the cooked *dals* and *kabuli chana*, the ginger-garlic paste, jaggery and ground *masala*; stir well and cook for one minute. Add half a cup of water, and bring to a boil. Lower the heat and simmer for ten minutes. Stir in the lemon juice and serve hot.

BANJARI DAL

This thick dal is wonderful with rotis and will take you back to the time of the Rajputana royals returning to camp after a good hunt.

Ingredients

- ⅔ cup black gram with skin (*chilkewali urad dal*), soaked
- ⅓ cup split Bengal gram (*chana dal*), soaked
- ¼ teaspoon turmeric powder
- Salt to taste
- 1½ tablespoons pure *ghee*
- 2 small onions, sliced
- 2 cloves
- 1 inch cinnamon
- 3 dried red chillies, broken into large bits
- 1½ teaspoons ginger-garlic paste
- 1½ teaspoons coriander powder
- 2 green chillies, chopped
- ¼ teaspoon black pepper powder
- ¾ teaspoon red chilli powder
- 1 tablespoon chopped fresh coriander leaves
- 1 inch ginger, cut into thin strips

Method

1. Pressure-cook the *urad dal* and *chana dal* together with the turmeric powder, salt and three cups of water till the pressure is released four or five times (four or five whistles), or till tender.
2. Heat the *ghee* in a separate pan; add the onions, cloves, cinnamon and red chillies and sauté till the onions turn golden.
3. Add the ginger-garlic paste, coriander powder, green chillies, pepper powder and chilli powder and sauté for a couple of minutes. Pour the sizzling spices over the cooked *dal* and cook for five minutes.
4. Garnish with the coriander leaves and ginger strips and serve hot.

GUJARATI KADHI

Who would have thought that a sweetish kadhi could be such a perfect accompaniment to pulaos and plain rice?
I can drink a few bowls of this as it is thin in consistency and quite a digestive aid. My only recommendation is that you have it piping hot.

Ingredients

¼ cup gram flour (*besan*)
2 cups yogurt
1 lemon-sized piece of jaggery, grated
2 green chillies, chopped
Salt to taste
2 tablespoons oil
½ teaspoon mustard seeds
½ teaspoon cumin seeds
8–10 curry leaves
2 dried red chillies, broken into large bits
3–4 cloves
1 inch cinnamon
⅛ teaspoon asafoetida (*hing*)

Method

1. Whisk together the *besan* and yogurt till smooth. Add four cups of water and mix well. Add the jaggery and green chillies.
2. Place the mixture in a pan and cook, stirring continuously, till the *kadhi* attains a moderately thick consistency. Add salt to taste.
3. Heat the oil in a small pan; add the mustard seeds, cumin seeds, curry leaves, red chillies, cloves, cinnamon and asafoetida. When the mustard seeds begin to splutter, pour the sizzling spices into the *kadhi* and mix well.
4. Serve hot.

SAMBHAR

There would probably be as many recipes of sambhar as there are households in South India! Every family has its own recipe, its own secret masala... try out this recipe and then start work on customising your own recipe!

Ingredients

½ cup split pigeon peas (*toovar/arhar dal*), soaked
¼ teaspoon turmeric powder
4 tablespoons sesame (*til*) oil
1 lemon-sized ball tamarind
½ teaspoon mustard seeds
4 dried red chillies, broken into large bits
½ teaspoon fenugreek seeds (*methi dana*), optional
¼ teaspoon asafoetida (*hing*)
4 green chillies, slit
10–12 curry leaves
2 drumsticks, cut into 2½-inch pieces
1½ teaspoons *sambhar* powder
Salt to taste
1 teaspoon rice flour
¼ cup chopped fresh coriander leaves

Chef's Tip:

You can use assorted vegetables like white radish (mooli), ladies' fingers (bhindi), pumpkin, brinjal (baingan), sambhar onions, etc., either individually or in any combination.

Method

1. Pressure-cook the *dal* in two and a half cups of water with turmeric powder and one teaspoon oil till the pressure is released two or three times (two or three whistles). Remove the lid once the pressure has reduced. Mash the cooked *dal* lightly with the back of a ladle.
2. Soak the tamarind in one cup of warm water; squeeze out the pulp, strain and set aside.
3. Heat the remaining oil in a thick-bottomed pan and add the mustard seeds. When they begin to splutter, add the red chillies, fenugreek seeds and asafoetida. Stir to mix.
4. Add the green chillies, curry leaves and drumsticks and cook for one minute over a medium heat, stirring now and then.
5. Add the tamarind pulp, *sambhar* powder, salt and one cup of water. Lower the heat and simmer for six to eight minutes, or till the drumsticks are tender. Add the boiled dal and simmer for two or three minutes.
6. Mix the rice flour into one-fourth cup of water and stir into the *sambhar*. Cook for another two or three minutes, stirring occasionally.
7. Sprinkle coriander leaves and serve hot.

LACHKO

For the uninitiated, relishing this mashed dal will take some deliberate effort but believe me, when made right this dal is delicious with rice and ghee, all blended with either kadhi or osaman.

Ingredients

1 cup split pigeon peas (*toovar dal/arhar dal*), soaked

½ teaspoon turmeric powder

Salt to taste

4–5 tablespoons pure *ghee*

Chef's Tip:

Lachko should be served with rice and Osaman (*page 26*)

Method

1. Pressure-cook the *dal* with the turmeric powder in two cups of water till the pressure is released three or four times (three or four whistles).
2. Remove the lid when the pressure reduces completely. Stir in the salt and one tablespoon of *ghee*. Bring the *dal* to a boil, lower heat and simmer for five minutes. Stir briskly.
3. Serve hot with the remaining *ghee* drizzled on top.

OSAMAN

Thin and watery, osaman is soothing for both the throat and stomach. I like both versions: moong and toovar dal so we cook them alternately at home. I enjoy it hot and steaming after a hard day's work.

Ingredients

1 cup whole green gram (*sabut moong*)
Salt to taste
½ inch ginger
2 green chillies
2 tablespoons oil
A large pinch of asafoetida (*hing*)
½ teaspoon mustard seeds
½ teaspoon cumin seeds
3–4 cloves
1 inch cinnamon
5–6 black peppercorns
12 curry leaves
½ teaspoon turmeric powder
2 tablespoons grated jaggery
1 tablespoon lemon juice
1 tablespoon chopped fresh coriander leaves

Chef's Tip:

Traditionally, osaman *is made with* toovar dal *but in my home it is made with* sabut moong. *Both are equally tasty.*

Method

1. Wash the *moong* and soak in two cups of water for about half an hour. Drain, add five cups of fresh water and salt and bring to a boil. Lower the heat and simmer until the *moong* is cooked. You can also pressure-cook the *moong* with five cups of water till the pressure is released four times (four whistles).
2. Strain the cooked *moong* and reserve the cooking liquid for this recipe. Use the *moong* to make any other dish.
3. Grind the ginger and green chillies to a fine paste. Stir one tablespoon of water into the paste.
4. Heat the oil in a pan; add the asafoetida, mustard seeds, cumin seeds, cloves, cinnamon, peppercorns, curry leaves, ginger-green chilli paste and salt.
5. When the seeds splutter, add the *moong* stock and stir. Add the turmeric powder and stir again. Adjust salt and add the jaggery.
6. Just before serving add the lemon juice and coriander leaves. Serve hot.

DAL CHENCHKI

Panch phoron is the famous spice used in most of the cooking in the eastern regions of the country.
This dal requires a little practice to perfect, as with the first few attempts you may get a mushy product – blame it on the masoor dal as it does cook fast!

Ingredients

1 cup split red lentils (*masoor dal*)
2 tablespoons pure *ghee*
8–10 baby onions, peeled
½ teaspoon cumin seeds
¼ teaspoon *paanch phoron* (see Note)
1 medium tomato, chopped
1 teaspoon red chilli powder
½ teaspoon turmeric powder
Salt to taste
½ teaspoon sugar
2 tablespoons chopped fresh coriander leaves

Note:

Paanch Phoron is a mixture of equal quantities of cumin seeds, mustard seeds, fennel seeds (saunf), fenugreek seeds (methi dana) and onion seeds (kalonji).

Method

1. Soak the *dal* in three cups of water for fifteen minutes. Drain, spread out on a large *thal* or plate and leave to dry.
2. Heat the *ghee* in a *kadai*; add the baby onions and fry lightly till brown. Add the cumi seeds, *paanch phoron*, tomato, chilli powder, turmeric powder and salt and sauté for two minutes.
3. Add the *dal* and sugar with one cup of water. Cover and continue cooking over a medium heat. Make sure that the *dal* remains whole and is not mashed. Garnish with coriander leaves and serve hot. The dish should be dry with practically no gravy.

MASALEDAR RANGOON VAAL

Nutritious dried broad field beans that are as soft as butter when cooked... make sure that you enjoy these on a holiday because you need time to cook them, relish them, and then to digest them!

Ingredients

2 cups broad field beans (*Rangoon vaal*), soaked overnight
¼ teaspoon soda bicarbonate
3 tablespoons oil
¼ teaspoon carom seeds (*ajwain*)
3–4 garlic cloves, chopped
A pinch of asafoetida (*hing*)
¼ teaspoon turmeric powder
1½ teaspoons red chilli powder
2 medium onions, ground to a paste
1 tablespoon grated jaggery
1 teaspoon tamarind pulp
Salt to taste

Method

1. Pressure-cook the *vaal* with the soda bicarbonate and four cups water till the pressure is released three or four times (three or four whistles).
2. Heat the oil in a pan; add the carom seeds, garlic, asafoetida, turmeric powder and chilli powder and stir for one minute.
3. Add the ground onions and sauté for two minutes.
4. Add the cooked *vaal* with one cup of water, the jaggery, tamarind pulp and salt and mix well.
5. Bring the mixture to a boil, lower the heat and simmer for five minutes. Serve hot.

SABZIYON WALI DAL

A dal and vegetable stew that is best eaten hot because it thickens fast thanks to the addition of leafy vegetables like arbi leaves.
I enjoy it more with brown rice than with rotis...

Ingredients

½ cup split pigeon peas (*toovar/arhar dal*), soaked

2 tablespoons split Bengal gram (*chana dal*), soaked

100 grams red pumpkin (*kaddu/laal bhopla*), diced

1 small brinjal (*baingan*), diced

1 small potato, diced

1 small bunch colocasia (*arbi*) leaves, chopped

¼ teaspoon turmeric powder

Salt to taste

1 tablespoon grated jaggery

1 tablespoon tamarind pulp

1 tablespoon chopped fresh coriander leaves

Seasoning

2 tablespoons oil

2 teaspoons mustard seeds

2 cloves

2 one-inch sticks cinnamon

1 dried red chilli, broken into large bits

½ teaspoon red chilli powder

¼ teaspoon asafoetida (*hing*)

Method

1. Pressure-cook the *dals* with the turmeric powder, salt and one and a half cups of water till the pressure is released three times (three whistles), or till the *dals* are soft. Mash the *dals* with the back of a ladle.
2. Boil the vegetables and colocasia leaves in one and a half cups of water till tender. Drain.
3. Add the cooked vegetables and colocasia leaves to the mashed *dal*. Mash again with the back of the ladle.
4. For the seasoning, heat the oil in a pan; add the mustard seeds, cloves, cinnamon, red chilli, chilli powder and asafoetida and sauté for one minute. Pour into the vegetable-*dal* mixture.
5. Add the jaggery and tamarind pulp and stir to mix. Bring the mixture to a boil, lower heat and simmer for five minutes. Serve hot, garnished with coriander leaves.

RAJASTHANI BAATI KI DAL

I would rate this dal with a ten on ten because this is what makes the baati so famous! However, in case you want to give the baati a miss, do have this dal with rice or roti. It will still be a winning combination.

Ingredients

½ cup split green gram (*dhuli moong dal*), soaked
5 tablespoons split Bengal gram (*chana dal*), soaked
Salt to taste
1 teaspoon turmeric powder
2 one-inch pieces ginger, chopped
2 tablespoons pure *ghee*
1 teaspoon cumin seeds
A pinch of asafoetida (*hing*)
3 dried red chillies, broken into large bits
1 large onion, chopped
1 tablespoon red chilli powder
1½ teaspoons dried mango powder (*amchur*)

Method

1. Boil the *dals* in four cups of water with the salt, turmeric powder and ginger till cooked.
2. Heat the *ghee* in a pan; add the cumin seeds, asafoetida and red chillies. When the cumin seeds begin to change colour, add the onion and sauté till light brown.
3. Add the chilli powder and cooked *dal* and mix well. Add half a cup of water and bring the mixture to a boil. Lower the heat and simmer for ten minutes. Add the *amchur* and stir to mix.
4. Serve hot with Rajasthani *baati* (baked balls of dough).

SINDHI KADHI

Full of vegetables that complement each other in taste, texture and colour, this kadhi is a visual delight. I recommend that you make only as much as will be consumed because it does not take refrigeration well.

Ingredients

½ cup split pigeon peas (*toovar/arhar dal*)
3 medium tomatoes, halved
3 tablespoons oil
¾ teaspoon cumin seeds
¼ teaspoon fenugreek seeds (*methi dana*)
A pinch of asafoetida (*hing*), optional
3 tablespoons gram flour (*besan*)
6–8 small ladies' fingers (*bhindi*), slit
2–3 green chillies, slit
10–12 cluster beans (*gawar*)
Salt to taste
1 teaspoon red chilli powder
¼ teaspoon turmeric powder
2 tablespoons tamarind pulp
7–8 curry leaves

Method

1. Soak the *toovar dal* in two cups of water for about half an hour. Drain.
2. Pressure-cook the *dal* with the tomatoes and two cups of water for three minutes, or till done. Remove the lid when the pressure has reduced completely. Mash the *dal* well and pass through a strainer pressing the *dal* through with the back of a ladle.
3. Heat one tablespoon of oil in a thick-bottomed pan. Add half a teaspoon of cumin seeds, the fenugreek seeds and asafoetida. When the cumin seeds begin to change colour, add the *besan* and sauté for about five minutes. Add three cups of water, a little at a time, stirring continuously to prevent lumps from forming.
4. Heat one tablespoon of oil in a separate pan. Add the ladies' fingers and sauté for one or two minutes.
5. Add the green chillies and cluster beans and continue to sauté for two or three minutes.
6. Add the mashed *toovar dal*, salt, chilli powder and turmeric powder to the *besan* mixture and mix well. Add a little water to the tamarind pulp and stir it into the *kadhi*. Add the sautéed vegetables and mix.
7. In a separate small pan, heat the remaining oil; add the remaining cumin seeds and curry leaves. When the cumin seeds change colour, pour the seasoning into the *kadhi*. Serve hot with steamed rice.

MOONG AUR HARE LASUN KI DAL

Imagine a chilly day and the need for some comfort food? Green gram with green garlic is perfect...
Use a few drops of lemon juice just before serving for that extra zing.

Ingredients

¾ cup whole green gram (*sabut moong*), soaked
½ cup chopped fresh green garlic (*hara lasun*)
¼ teaspoon turmeric powder
Salt to taste
2 tablespoons oil
½ teaspoon cumin seeds
1 teaspoon ginger-garlic paste
1 teaspoon green chilli paste
A pinch of asafoetida (*hing*)
2 medium tomatoes, chopped
1 tablespoon chopped fresh coriander leaves

Method

1. Pressure-cook the *moong* with the turmeric powder, salt and three cups of water till the pressure is released twice (two whistles). Set aside.
2. Heat the oil in a thick-bottomed pan and add the cumin seeds. When they begin to change colour, add the ginger-garlic paste, green chilli paste and asafoetida and sauté for one minute.
3. Add the green garlic and sauté for another minute. Add the tomatoes and sauté till the oil separates.
4. Add the cooked *dal* and half a cup of water and bring to a boil. Lower the heat and simmer for two minutes.
5. Garnish with coriander leaves and serve hot.

TOMATO RASAM

Call it rasam, chaaru or saaru in any south Indian language – the recipe will have the imprint of the cook!
This recipe relies heavily on tomatoes for the sour flavour. Rasam can be served with rice or had by itself as an appetiser.

Ingredients

4 tablespoons split pigeon peas (*arhar/toovar dal*)
½ lemon-sized ball tamarind
¼ cup fresh coriander leaves, chopped
1½ teaspoons *rasam* powder
¼ teaspoon asafoetida (*hing*)
Salt to taste
10–12 curry leaves
2 medium tomatoes, chopped
4 tablespoons pure *ghee*
½ teaspoon mustard seeds
2 dried red chillies

Chef's Tip:

To serve rasam as an appetiser, strain and pour into small glasses, garnished with a slice of lemon. Traditionally, rasam *is cooked in a pan made from a special alloy, which gives the* rasam *its unique flavour.*

Method

1. Wash, drain and cook the *toovar dal* in two cups of water until soft. Strain and mash well. Reserve the strained cooking liquid.
2. Soak the tamarind in one cup of warm water; squeeze out the pulp, strain and reserve.
3. Reserve some chopped coriander leaves to garnish. Mix the tamarind pulp with remaining chopped coriander leaves, *rasam* powder, asafoetida, salt and half the quantity of curry leaves. Bring to a boil, lower heat and simmer for two or three minutes.
4. Add the chopped tomatoes and the reserved cooking liquid. Simmer for four or five minutes and stir in the mashed *dal* and cook for another minute.
5. Remove from heat and sprinkle the reserved chopped coriander leaves.
6. Heat the *ghee* in a small pan; add the mustard seeds and sauté till they begin to splutter. Add the red chillies and remaining curry leaves and stir well. Pour the sizzling spices over the *rasam* and cover immediately to trap the flavours. Serve hot.

DAL DHOKLI

Talk about a perfect one-pot meal on a cool evening... that is Dal Dhokli for you!
I call it 'Indian pasta'.
The peanuts add an interesting texture to the soft dal and dhokli.

Ingredients

¾ cup split pigeon peas (*arhar/toovar dal*)
¾ cup wholewheat flour (*atta*)
2 tablespoons gram flour (*besan*)
Salt to taste
¾ teaspoon turmeric powder
¾ teaspoon red chilli powder
2 pinches asafoetida (*hing*)
½ tablespoon oil
1 ½ tablespoons peanuts
1 tablespoon *ghee*
¼ teaspoon mustard seeds
½ teaspoon cumin seeds
4 garlic cloves, peeled and finely chopped
4 curry leaves
3 pieces of *kokum*
1 ½ teaspoons grated jaggery
2 tablespoons chopped fresh coriander leaves

Method

1. Soak the *toovar dal* in two cups of water for half an hour.
2. Mix together the wholewheat flour and gram flour. Add salt, one-fourth teaspoon turmeric powder, chilli powder, a pinch of asafoetida, oil and enough water to make a stiff dough. Roll the dough out into thin *rotis* and cut into desired shapes (*dhokli*).
3. Boil the *dal* with one and a half cups of water. When the *dal* is half-cooked, add the peanuts and remaining turmeric powder.
4. Heat the *ghee* in a pan; add the mustard seeds, cumin seeds, remaining asafoetida, garlic and curry leaves and sauté for a few seconds. Pour the sizzling spices into the *dal*.
5. Add two cups of water and the *kokum* to the *dal* and bring to a boil; stir in the jaggery.
6. Add the strips of dough and cook, stirring occasionally, so that the *dhokli* do not stick to the bottom of the pan.
7. Adjust salt and serve hot, garnished with chopped coriander leaves.

LAUKI CHANA DAL

This dal is made differently in different homes. I prefer the slightly watery one as it is good with rice. Some prefer to add jaggery instead of sugar and kokum instead of lemon juice.

Ingredients

- ½ small bottle gourd (*lauki*), cut into 1-inch pieces
- ½ cup split Bengal gram (*chana dal*)
- Salt to taste
- ½ teaspoon turmeric powder
- 1 tablespoon oil
- ½ teaspoon cumin seeds
- 2 green chillies, chopped
- A pinch of asafoetida (*hing*)
- ½ teaspoon red chilli powder
- 2 teaspoons coriander powder
- 2 medium tomatoes, chopped
- ½ teaspoon *garam masala* powder
- ¼ teaspoon sugar
- 2 teaspoons lemon juice
- 2 tablespoons chopped fresh coriander leaves

Method

1. Soak the *chana dal* in one and half cups of water for one hour. Drain.
2. Cook the *chana dal* and *lauki* with salt, turmeric powder and one cup of water till soft. Mash slightly with the back of ladle and mix well.
3. Heat the oil in a separate pan. Add the cumin seeds, green chillies and asafoetida and cook for one minute. Add the chilli powder and coriander powder and cook till fragrant.
4. Add the tomatoes and cook till they soften.
5. Add the cooked *chana dal* and *lauki* and stir to mix. Add the *garam masala* powder, sugar and more salt if necessary. Lower the heat and cook for two minutes.
6. Stir in the lemon juice, garnish with coriander leaves and serve hot.

ARBI KI KADHI

A wonderful gravy dish to have with rajgira puris on a fasting day. For everyday meals you can substitute water chestnut flour with gram flour. But let me tell you the version given here is tastier!

Ingredients

250 grams colocasia (*arbi*), boiled
2 tablespoons oil + for deep-frying
¼ cup water chestnut flour (*singhare ka atta*)
1½ cups sour yogurt
Rock salt (*sendha namak*) to taste
1 teaspoon red chilli powder
½ teaspoon turmeric powder
½ teaspoon cumin seeds
2–3 dried red chillies, broken into large bits
1 tablespoon chopped fresh coriander leaves

Chef's Tip:

You can also make aloo ki kadhi *by substituting potatoes for the* arbi.

Method

1. Cool the *arbi* slightly, peel and cut into half-inch thick slices.
2. Heat the oil in a *kadai* and deep-fry the *arbi* till golden brown. Drain on absorbent paper.
3. Whisk the water chestnut flour into the yogurt till smooth. Add the rock salt, chilli powder and turmeric powder and mix again. Add two cups of water and whisk well.
4. Heat two tablespoons of oil in a deep pan; add the cumin seeds and red chillies. When the cumin seeds begin to change colour, stir in the yogurt mixture. Cook for five minutes, stirring continuously.
5. Add the fried *arbi* and mix. Continue cooking for five more minutes or till you get the desired consistency. Garnish with coriander leaves and serve hot.

SINDHI DAL

I particularly like this dal because amchur and curry leaves blend perfectly to give it a unique flavour... skimp on neither as the final taste depends on them.

Ingredients

1 cup split Bengal gram (*chana dal*)

Salt to taste

¼ teaspoon turmeric powder

½ teaspoon red chilli powder

¼ teaspoon *garam masala* powder

¾ teaspoon dried mango powder (*amchur*)

3 tablespoons oil

1 teaspoon cumin seeds

4–5 green chillies, slit

8–10 curry leaves

1 medium onion, chopped

½ cup chopped fresh coriander leaves

Method

1. Soak the *chana dal* in three cups of water for about one hour. Drain and cook with three cups of water, salt and turmeric powder till just done.
2. Heat a pan; add the cooked *dal* and half a cup of water if the *dal* is too dry. Stir and add half the chilli powder, half the *garam masala* powder, the *amchur* and more salt if necessary. Stir gently and cook over a low heat.
3. Heat the oil in a separate pan and add the cumin seeds. When they begin to change colour, add the green chillies, curry leaves, remaining *garam masala* powder and remaining chilli powder. Stir and add the sizzling spices to the *dal*. Mix well and take the pan off the heat.
4. Garnish with the chopped onion and coriander leaves and serve hot.

TITTORI

Coconut milk adds a creamy consistency and delicate flavour to this Parsi dal. You can also include green chilli paste in which case, the dal gets a pleasant green hue. You can use garam masala instead of dhansak masala.

Ingredients

1 ½ cups broad field beans (*vaal*), sprouted and peeled
1 ¼ tablespoons Parsi *dhansak masala*
2 tablespoons oil
2 large onions, chopped
2 teaspoons ginger-garlic paste
¼ teaspoon turmeric powder
¾ teaspoon *garam masala* powder
1 ½ teaspoons red chilli powder
1 ½ teaspoons sugar
Salt to taste
2 large tomatoes, chopped
1 ½ cups thick coconut milk

Method

1. Heat the oil in a thick-bottomed pan; add the onions and ginger-garlic paste and sauté till the onions turn translucent.
2. Add the *dhansak masala*, turmeric powder, *garam masala* powder, chilli powder, sugar, salt and tomatoes; sauté till the oil separates.
3. Add the *vaal* and one-and-a-half cups of water and bring to a boil. Lower the heat and simmer till the *vaal* is completely cooked.
4. Gently stir in the coconut milk, so that the beans do not break. Simmer for two more minutes. Serve hot.

TURAI MASOOR

Ghee plays a major role in giving this dal its flavour. For a variation, use soya nuggets instead of turai.

Ingredients

500 grams ridge gourd (*turai*), peeled and chopped
1 cup whole lentile (*sabut masoor*), soaked
¼ teaspoon turmeric powder
Salt to taste
3 tablespoons pure *ghee*
2 medium onions, chopped
1 teaspoon cumin seeds
1 teaspoon ginger-garlic paste
2 teaspoons coriander powder
A pinch of asafoetida (*hing*)
1½ teaspoons red chilli powder
1 teaspoon *garam masala* powder
2 tablespoons chopped fresh coriander leaves

Method

1. Pressure-cook the *masoor* with turmeric powder, salt and three cups of water till the pressure is released two or three times (two or three whistles). Lightly mash the *masoor* with the back of a ladle.
2. Heat one tablespoon of *ghee* in a pan; add the onions and sauté till translucent.
3. Add the *turai*, salt and half a cup of water. Cover and cook over a medium heat till the *turai* is tender.
4. Add the cooked *masoor* and approximately half a cup of water. Adjust seasoning and bring the mixture to a boil. Remove from heat and set aside.
5. For the seasoning, heat the remaining *ghee* in a small pan; add the cumin seeds, ginger-garlic paste, coriander powder, asafoetida, chilli powder and *garam masala* powder and sauté till the spices begin to sizzle.
6. Pour the seasoning over the *masoor*. Serve hot, garnished with coriander leaves.

RAJASTHANI KADHI

The addition of ajwain in the pakore gives the kadhi its regional flavour. Ensure that the yogurt is sour for best results.

Ingredients

Pakore

1 cup gram flour (*besan*)

A pinch of soda bicarbonate

2 green chillies, chopped

½ teaspoon red chilli powder

½ teaspoon carom seeds (*ajwain*)

½ teaspoon turmeric powder

½ teaspoon coriander powder

Salt to taste

Oil for deep-frying

Kadhi

2 cups sour yogurt

2 tablespoons gram flour (*besan*)

Salt to taste

¾ teaspoon turmeric powder

1 tablespoon oil

½ teaspoon cumin seeds

A pinch of asafoetida (*hing*)

2–3 green chillies, chopped

1 inch ginger, chopped

10-12 curry leaves

½ teaspoon red chilli powder

Method

1. For the *pakore*, mix all the ingredients, except the oil, with one-fourth cup of water.
2. Heat the oil in a *kadai*; drop small portions of the *pakore* mixture into the hot oil and deep-fry till golden brown. Drain on absorbent paper and set aside.
3. For the *kadhi*, mix together the yogurt, *besan*, salt and turmeric powder and whisk well till smooth.
4. Heat one tablespoon of oil in a *kadai* and add the cumin seeds. When they begin to change colour, add the asafoetida, green chillies and ginger and sauté for one minute.
5. Add the curry leaves, chilli powder and the yogurt mixture. Bring to a boil and cook, stirring continuously, till thick.
6. Stir in the *pakore* and serve hot with rice.

MAA CHOLE DI DAL

Some people prefer to add a large bit of hing in this dal as it is heavy to digest. The best result is obtained if you soak the dals well. They blend with the masalas better.

Ingredients

½ cup split black gram (*chilkewali urad dal*)
½ cup split Bengal gram (*chana dal*)
Salt to taste
¼ teaspoon turmeric powder
1 inch ginger, chopped
3 green chillies, chopped
2–3 tablespoons pure *ghee*
1 tablespoon butter
1 teaspoon cumin seeds
1 medium onion, chopped
2 medium tomatoes, chopped
½ teaspoon red chilli powder
2 tablespoons chopped fresh coriander leaves

Method

1. Mix the two *dals*, wash and soak in four cups of water for one hour. Drain.
2. Place the soaked *dals* in a pan with four cups of water, salt to taste, turmeric powder, half the ginger and half the green chillies. Cover and cook over a low heat till the *dals* are tender. Stir well with a ladle to mix well without mashing the *dals*.
3. Heat the *ghee* and butter in a pan; add the cumin seeds, remaining green chillies and ginger. Stir and add the onion and sauté till light brown.
4. Add the tomatoes and sauté till they soften. Add the chilli powder and sauté for half a minute.
5. Add the sizzling seasoning to the *dal* and mix well. Simmer for a few minutes and serve hot, garnished with the coriander leaves.

KHATTI MEETHI DAL

In some Gujarati homes, this sweet and sour dal is a daily requirement! No, it is not boring to have it because it can be made with slight variations like the addition of sem ki phalli, or eliminating the peanuts. It tastes particularly good with cooked rice and a dollop of ghee.

Ingredients

1 cup split pigeon peas (*toovar/arhar dal*)
¼ teaspoon asafoetida (*hing*)
½ teaspoon crushed fenugreek seeds (*methi dana*)
1 medium tomato, chopped
½ teaspoon green chilli-ginger paste
7–8 curry leaves
½ teaspoon turmeric powder
½ teaspoon red chilli powder
¼ teaspoon coriander powder
¼ teaspoon cumin powder
Salt to taste
3–4 pieces *kokum*
2 tablespoons grated jaggery
½ cup raw peanuts
1 tablespoon chopped fresh coriander leaves

Seasoning

1 tablespoon oil
1 dried red button chilli (*bor mirchi*)
½ teaspoon mustard seeds
½ teaspoon cumin seeds
A pinch of asafoetida (*hing*)

Chef's Tip:

You can add chopped kharak *(dried dates) for added texture and taste.*

Method

1. Soak the *dal* in two cups of water for one hour. Drain and pressure-cook in three cups of water with the asafoetida and *methi dana* till the pressure is released four times (four whistles). Remove the lid when the pressure has completely reduced.
2. Transfer the *dal* to a thick-bottomed pan. Add one and a half cups of water and the tomato. Process with a hand blender till smooth.
3. Place on heat and add the green chilli-ginger paste, curry leaves, turmeric powder, chilli powder, coriander and cumin powders, salt, *kokum*, jaggery and peanuts, one by one, stirring continuously.
4. Bring to a boil, lower heat and simmer for twelve to fifteen minutes. Adjust the consistency by adding water if needed. Remove from heat and sprinkle with the coriander leaves. Do not stir the leaves into the *dal*.
5. For the seasoning, heat the oil in a small pan; add the *bor mirchi*, mustard seeds and cumin seeds. When the mustard seeds begin to splutter, add the asafoetida and immediately pour over the coriander leaves. This ensures that the coriander leaves remain green. Cover the pan with a lid immediately to trap the flavours.
6. Place the pan on heat again and bring to a boil. Adjust the consistency and salt. Serve hot with rice.

DHANSAK DAL

This is the Sunday special in a Parsi home. But why not include it in your repertoire, for it is loaded with the goodness of various dals and vegetables? This dish is prepared in a different manner in different households and for many the recipe of the special dhansak masala is a closely-guarded secret.

Ingredients

2 teaspoons split red lentils (*masoor dal*), soaked

2 teaspoons split green gram (*dhuli moong dal*), soaked

2 teaspoons split black gram (*dhuli urad dal*), soaked

2 teaspoons split broad field beans (*vaal dal*), soaked

3 tablespoons split pigeon peas (*toovar/arhar dal*), soaked

1 small potato, peeled and chopped

1 small brinjal, chopped

1 small bottle gourd (*doodhi/lauki*), peeled and chopped

1 tablespoon chopped fresh fenugreek leaves (*methi*)

1 medium tomato, chopped

2–3 spring onions, chopped

1 lemon-sized ball tamarind

3 tablespoons oil

Salt to taste

2 teaspoons chopped fresh coriander leaves

Masala

1 green chilli

2 dried red chillies

4 garlic cloves

1 inch cinnamon

4 cloves

1 inch ginger

1 green cardamom

1 teaspoon coriander seeds

4 black peppercorns

½ teaspoon cumin seeds

Masala Powder

1 green cardamom

1 inch cinnamon

1 clove

Method

1. Pressure-cook the *dals* together with all the vegetables, except the spring onions, with three cups of water till the pressure is released three times (three whistles). Set aside to cool. Purée the mixture in a blender.
2. Grind all the ingredients for the *masala* with a little water to a fine paste. Grind all the ingredients for the *masala* powder to a fine powder.
3. Soak the tamarind in one-fourth cup of water. Strain the pulp.
4. Heat the oil in a *kadai*; add the spring onions and sauté for one minute. Add the ground *masala* paste and sauté for two minutes.
5. Add the *dal* and vegetable purée, salt, *masala* powder and tamarind pulp and bring to a boil. Lower heat and simmer for ten to fifteen minutes.
6. Serve hot, garnished with coriander leaves.

LEELI TOOVAR NI KADHI

Fresh, tender toovar beans are available only in the winter months. Enterprising Gujaratis store them in the freezer for use all year round.

Ingredients

½ cup fresh green pigeon peas (*leeli toovar*), boiled and drained

4 tablespoons gram flour (*besan*)

2 cups yogurt

2 tablespoons pure *ghee*

1 teaspoon carom seeds (*ajwain*)

4 dried red button chillies (*bor mirchi*)

1 inch ginger, chopped

2 teaspoons garlic paste

3 green chillies, chopped

8–10 curry leaves

A pinch of asafoetida (*hing*)

2 medium brinjals (*baingan*), diced

Salt to taste

2 teaspoons sugar

1 tablespoon chopped fresh *coriander leaves*

Method

1. Whisk the *besan* and yogurt together. Add four cups of water and whisk till smooth.
2. Heat the *ghee* in a deep pan; add the carom seeds, *bor mirchi*, ginger, garlic, green chillies and curry leaves and sauté for two minutes. Add the asafoetida and brinjals and sauté for two minutes.
3. Add the boiled *toovar* and sauté for one minute. Stir in the yogurt mixture and bring the mixture to a boil. Add the salt and sugar, lower heat and simmer, stirring gently, for ten to fifteen minutes, or till thickened to the desired consistency.
4. Add the coriander leaves and serve hot.

PALAK KI KADHI

A healthier, tastier version of the humble kadhi. This recipe is especially handy when you desire to serve something new and different with rice.

Ingredients

½ medium bunch (100 grams) spinach (*palak*), chopped
2 cups yogurt, whisked
4 tablespoons gram flour (*besan*)
2 tablespoons oil
1 teaspoon cumin seeds
½ teaspoon fenugreek seeds (*methi dana*)
A pinch of asafoetida (*hing*)
1 large onion, chopped
1 teaspoon ginger paste
3 green chillies, chopped
¼ teaspoon turmeric powder
½ teaspoon red chilli powder
Salt to taste
1 teaspoon sugar (optional)

Method

1. Whisk together the yogurt, *besan* and three cups of water till smooth.
2. Heat the oil in a non-stick pan and add the cumin seeds and fenugreek seeds. When the seeds begin to change colour, add the asafoetida and onion and sauté for two minutes.
3. Add the ginger paste and green chillies and sauté for half a minute. Add the turmeric powder, chilli powder and spinach and sauté for two minutes.
4. Add the yogurt mixture and bring to a boil. Add the salt and sugar, lower the heat and simmer for ten to fifteen minutes, or till the *kadhi* thickens. Serve hot.

DAL HARI BHARI

Getting my daughters to eat greens is no longer a problem as this dal is a terrific solution. There is no way they can pick out the palak and methi from it! In fact, I think this dal is a good healthy idea for the entire family.

Ingredients

1 cup split green gram (*dhuli moong dal*)

1 medium bunch (200 grams) fresh spinach leaves (*palak*), chopped

1 medium bunch (250 grams) fresh fenugreek leaves (*methi*), chopped

3 tablespoons chopped fresh coriander leaves

½ teaspoon turmeric powder

Salt to taste

6 garlic cloves, chopped

3 green chillies, chopped

1 inch ginger, chopped

2 tablespoons pure *ghee*

1 teaspoon cumin seeds

2 medium onions, chopped

2 medium tomatoes, chopped

¾ teaspoon red chilli powder

1 tablespoon lemon juice

Method

1. Soak the *dal* in two cups of water for one hour. Pressure-cook with the turmeric powder and salt till the pressure is released twice (two whistles). Remove the lid when the pressure has completely reduced and mash the *dal* with the back of a ladle.
2. Grind the garlic, green chillies and ginger to a paste.
3. Heat the *ghee* in a pan and add the cumin seeds. When the seeds begin to change colour, add the onions and sauté till light brown. Add the tomatoes, chilli powder and ground paste. Sauté till tomatoes soften.
4. Add the *palak*, *methi* and coriander leaves and sauté for four or five minutes.
5. Stir in the cooked *dal* and one cup of water and bring the mixture to a boil. Stir in the lemon juice.
6. Cook for four or five minutes, stirring continuously. Serve hot with rice.

METHIWALI ARHAR DAL

Thick and tasty, this dal is a treat for garlic lovers as it contains whole garlic cloves fried in ghee! They can be substituted with minced garlic but the final taste is not the same.

Ingredients

½ medium bunch (125 grams) fresh fenugreek (*methi*) leaves, chopped

1 cup split pigeon peas (*toovar/arhar dal*)

½ teaspoon turmeric powder

Salt to taste

½ teaspoon red chilli powder

1 teaspoon grated jaggery

Seasoning

1 tablespoon pure *ghee*

¼ teaspoon asafoetida (*hing*)

6 garlic cloves

Method

1. Soak the *dal* in two cups of water for one hour. Drain.
2. Pressure-cook in three cups of water with the turmeric powder till the pressure is released four times (four whistles). Remove the lid when the pressure reduces completely and mash the *dal* well with the back of a ladle.
3. Add half a cup of water, salt, the chilli powder and jaggery and bring to a boil.
4. For the seasoning, heat the *ghee* in a small pan; add the asafoetida and the garlic cloves. Sauté till the garlic turns light brown.
5. Add the *methi* and sauté for one or two minutes. Pour the seasoning over the *dal* and stir well. Adjust the consistency by adding water if necessary.
6. Serve hot.

GANTHIA NI KADHI

When you want to make a kadhi with a deliberate twist add ganthia! It is a handy snack to have in the house as it can be converted into an instant vegetable with onions and tomatoes.

Ingredients

2 cups *Bhavnagri ganthia*

2 cups sour yogurt

½ teaspoon turmeric powder

1 teaspoon red chilli powder

3 tablespoons gram flour (*besan*)

Salt to taste

2 tablespoons oil

½ teaspoon mustard seeds

A pinch of asafoetida (*hing*)

Method

1. Whisk the yogurt with three cups of water, the turmeric powder, chilli powder, *besan* and salt till smooth.
2. Heat the oil in a *kadai* and add the mustard seeds. When they begin to splutter, add the asafoetida and the yogurt mixture.
3. Bring the *kadhi* to a boil, lower heat and simmer for eight to ten minutes, stirring continuously.
4. Stir in the *ganthia* and simmer for two more minutes. Serve hot with steamed rice.

PUNJABI RAJMA

This is one dish that reminds me of Saturday afternoons during my childhood... rajma with its gravy, garnished with fresh coriander, hot fluffy basmati rice and thinly sliced onions doused in lemon juice. No wonder it is still my favourite meal!

Ingredients

1½ cups red kidney beans (*rajma*), soaked overnight

3 tablespoons oil

2 bay leaves

2 medium onions, chopped

1 inch ginger, chopped

6–8 garlic cloves, chopped

2 teaspoons red chilli powder

1 tablespoon coriander powder

½ teaspoon turmeric powder

1 teaspoon cumin powder

3 medium tomatoes, chopped

Salt to taste

1 teaspoon *garam masala* powder

1 tablespoon chopped fresh coriander leaves

Method

1. Pressure-cook the *rajma* with five cups of water till the pressure is released five times (five whistles) or completely cooked and soft.
2. Heat the oil in a deep pan; add the bay leaves and onions and sauté till golden. Add the ginger and garlic and continue to sauté for one minute.
3. Add the chilli powder, coriander powder, turmeric powder, cumin powder and stir to mix. Add the tomatoes and salt and cook till tomatoes are cooked and the oil separates.
4. Add the *rajma* along with the cooking liquid and mix. Cook over a low heat for fifteen minutes, stirring occasionally. Add more salt if necessary and the *garam masala* powder. Cook for another five minutes.
5. Garnish with coriander leaves and serve hot with steamed rice.

BHINDA NI KADHI

Ensure that the bhindi are absolutely dry before you sauté them...
they will remain crisp when put into the kadhi.
This is a common summer recipe in Gujarati homes.

Ingredients

15 ladies' fingers (*bhinda/bhindi*), cut into ½-inch pieces

3 tablespoons oil

2 cups sour yogurt

4 tablespoons gram flour (*besan*)

½ teaspoon turmeric powder

1 teaspoon red chilli powder

Salt to taste

¾ teaspoon mustard seeds

½ teaspoon fenugreek seeds (*methi dana*)

5 garlic cloves, sliced

1 inch ginger, cut into thin strips

2 green chillies, chopped

¼ teaspoon asafoetida (*hing*)

2 tablespoons chopped fresh coriander leaves

Method

1. Heat two tablespoons of oil in a pan; add the *bhindi* and sauté till lightly browned.
2. Whisk together the yogurt, *besan*, turmeric powder, chilli powder and salt till smooth. Add four cups of water and whisk again.
3. Heat the remaining oil in a *kadai*; add the mustard seeds and fenugreek seeds. When they begin to splutter, add the garlic, ginger, green chillies and asafoetida and sauté for half a minute.
4. Add the yogurt mixture and bring to a boil. Lower heat and cook, stirring continuously, till quite thick.
5. Add the fried *bhindi* and simmer for two or three minutes. Garnish with coriander leaves and serve hot.

VRAT KI KADHI

The use of singhare ka atta makes this a delicious addition to fasting recipes. I like to make this kadhi even otherwise, as it is much lighter than the one with gram flour.

Ingredients

1¾ cups yogurt

2 tablespoons water chestnut flour (*singhare ka atta*)

¼ teaspoon rock salt (*sendha namak*)

1 teaspoon red chilli powder

¼ teaspoon cinnamon powder

2 tablespoons pure *ghee*

1 teaspoon cumin seeds

3–4 dried red chillies, broken into large bits

10–12 curry leaves

½ teaspoon sugar

Salt to taste

1 tablespoon chopped fresh coriander leaves

Method

1. Whisk together the yogurt, water chestnut flour, rock salt, chilli powder and cinnamon powder. Add four cups of water and mix well.
2. Heat the *ghee* in a *kadai*; add the cumin seeds, red chillies and curry leaves. Sauté till the cumin seeds begin to splutter.
3. Add the yogurt mixture and cook till the *kadhi* thickens slightly. Stir in the sugar and salt. Cook over a low heat for two minutes.
4. Garnish with coriander leaves and serve hot.

TUR DAL AMTI

The name indicates a sour dal and the presence of tamarind pulp makes it so. Do not skip the goda masala as that is the life and soul of this flavourful dish.

Ingredients

1 cup split pigeon peas (*toovar/arhar dal*), soaked

2 tablespoons oil

¼ teaspoon cumin seeds

1 small onion, chopped

2 green chillies

A pinch of asafoetida (*hing*)

Salt to taste

1 teaspoon grated jaggery

2 teaspoons tamarind pulp

½ teaspoon red chilli powder

½ teaspoon *goda masala*

1 tablespoon chopped fresh coriander leaves

1 tablespoon grated coconut

Method

1. Pressure-cook the *dal* with two cups of water till the pressure is released three or four times (three or four whistles). Remove the lid when the pressure has reduced completely. Mash the *dal* with the back of a ladle.
2. Heat the oil in a deep pan; add the cumin seeds and sauté till they begin to change colour. Add the onion, green chillies and asafoetida and sauté till lightly browned.
3. Add the cooked *dal* and two cups of water. Mix well and bring to a boil.
4. Lower the heat, add salt, the jaggery, tamarind pulp, chilli powder and *goda masala* and simmer for four or five minutes.
5. Garnish with coriander leaves and coconut and serve hot.

SOOKHI MOONG DAL

This recipe will come in handy when you are short of vegetables. Try this dal with thin Gujarati kadhi as an accompaniment. Then all the meal needs is a salad and roti.

Ingredients

1 ¼ cups split green gram (*dhuli moong dal*)

Salt to taste

½ teaspoon turmeric powder

3 tablespoons oil

½ teaspoon cumin seeds

A pinch of asafoetida (*hing*)

2 one-inch pieces ginger, chopped

1 green chilli, chopped

1 teaspoon red chilli powder

2 teaspoons lemon juice

1 tablespoon chopped fresh coriander leaves

Method

1. Soak the *dal* in two cups of water for half an hour. Boil the *dal* with salt and the turmeric powder till just cooked. Drain excess water, if any.
2. Heat the oil in a *kadai*; add the cumin seeds and asafoetida. When the cumin seeds begin to change colour, add the ginger and green chilli and sauté for half a minute.
3. Add the chilli powder and cooked *dal* and mix well. Stir in the lemon juice and more salt if necessary. Mix lightly, taking care not to mash the *dal*. Cook till dry.
4. Serve hot, garnished with coriander leaves.

DAL MAHARANI

I am transported to my student days when I would get back from college feeling ravenous. A bowlful of dal straight from the fridge with a couple of paranthe would be like manna from heaven. In fact, I used to get annoyed if Mom would reheat the leftover dal as I liked it cold.

Ingredients

½ cup whole black gram (*sabut urad*)

2 tablespoons red kidney beans (*rajma*)

Salt to taste

1 teaspoon red chilli powder

1½ inches ginger, chopped

1 tablespoon pure *ghee*

2 tablespoons butter

1 teaspoon cumin seeds

2 medium onions, chopped

10 garlic cloves, chopped

1 medium tomato, chopped

1 teaspoon *garam masala* powder

¼ cup cream (*malai*)

Chef's Tip:

This dish tastes just as good reheated the following day! But it also tastes delicious eaten cold with hot paranthe.

Method

1. Soak the *sabut urad* and *rajma* overnight in five cups of water. Drain.
2. Pressure-cook the soaked *sabut urad* and *rajma* in five cups of water with salt, the chilli powder and ginger till the pressure is released eight times (eight whistles).
3. Heat the *ghee* and butter in a thick-bottomed pan and add the cumin seeds. When they begin to change colour, add the onions and sauté till golden brown.
4. Add the garlic and tomato and sauté till the tomato is pulpy and the oil separates.
5. Add the boiled *sabut urad*, *rajma* and one cup of water and bring to a boil. Add the *garam masala* powder and cook over a very low heat for fifteen minutes. Stir in the cream and simmer for another five minutes.
6. Serve hot with *naan* or *parantha*.

MAHARASHTRIAN KADHI

If you love ginger and garlic, do increase the quantities to suit your taste. I find the proportions in the recipe just right!

Ingredients

4 tablespoons gram flour (*besan*)
3 cups yogurt
Salt to taste
1 teaspoon turmeric powder
1 tablespoon oil
½ teaspoon mustard seeds
2 teaspoons ginger paste
1 teaspoon garlic paste
2 green chillies, slit
A pinch of asafoetida (*hing*)
4–6 curry leaves
2 tablespoons chopped fresh coriander leaves

Method

1. Combine the *besan* and yogurt thoroughly in a deep pan. Add two cups of water, salt to taste and turmeric powder. Cook over a low heat stirring continuously.
2. Heat the oil in a separate pan and add the mustard seeds. When they begin to splutter add the ginger paste, garlic paste, green chillies, asafoetida and curry leaves. Cook for one minute and pour the sizzling spices into the *kadhi*.
3. Mix well and cook, stirring continuously, over a low heat until the *kadhi* has thickened slightly.
4. Remove from heat and serve, garnished with coriander leaves.

DHAABAY DI DAL

The taste develops as this dal sits. So make a rather large batch and freeze one portion. You can use it in an emergency or even the following day as the flavours are properly mingled.

Ingredients

½ cup black gram with skin (*chilkewali urad dal)*

¼ cup split Bengal gram (*chana dal*)

¼ cup red kidney beans (*rajma*)

4 tablespoons oil

8–10 garlic cloves, chopped

2 medium onions, chopped

2–3 green chillies, chopped

½ tablespoon roasted cumin powder

1 tablespoon red chilli powder

3 medium tomatoes, chopped

3 tablespoons butter

Salt to taste

2 tablespoons chopped fresh coriander leaves

1 tablespoon dried fenugreek leaves (*kasoori methi)*

Method

1. Soak the *urad dal*, *chana dal* and *rajma* in three cups of water for at least six hours.
2. Drain the soaked *dals*, add six cups of water and pressure-cook till the pressure is released eight times (eight whistles), or until the *dals* are completely cooked. Mix the *dals* well with a ladle.
3. Heat the oil in a pan; add the garlic and sauté for a few minutes till golden brown. Add the onions and green chillies and sauté for four or five minutes, or until the onions turn golden brown.
4. Add the cumin powder and chilli powder and sauté for a few seconds. Add the tomatoes and cook over a high heat for three or four minutes, stirring continuously. Stir in the cooked *dals* and butter and mix well.
5. Add the salt and coriander leaves and cook for ten minutes over a low heat, stirring occasionally.
6. Crush the *kasoori methi* between your palms, sprinkle over the *dal* and serve hot.

RAJASTHANI PANCHMEL DAL

Panchmel means mixture of five; in fact a happy mixture because the dals though so different in texture and taste, blend together to give a delicious mix.

Ingredients

¼ cup split Bengal gram (*chana dal*)
¼ cup whole green gram (*sabut moong*)
¼ cup split black gram (*dhuli urad dal*)
¼ cup split pigeon peas (*toovar/arhar dal*)
¼ cup whole red lentils (*sabut masoor*)
Salt to taste
½ teaspoon turmeric powder
3 tablespoons oil
A pinch of asafoetida (*hing*)
½ teaspoon cumin seeds
4–5 cloves
2 dried red chillies, broken into large bits
1 teaspoon green chilli-ginger paste
1 teaspoon roasted cumin powder
1 teaspoon coriander powder
½ teaspoon red chilli powder
2 medium tomatoes, chopped
½ teaspoon *garam masala* powder
2 tablespoons chopped fresh coriander leaves

Method

1. Soak the *dals* in three cups of water for at least two hours. Drain and boil in three cups of water with salt and the turmeric powder till done.
2. Heat the oil in a pan; add the asafoetida, cumin seeds, cloves and red chillies. When the cumin seeds begin to change colour, add the green chilli-ginger paste and sauté for one minute.
3. Add the cumin powder, coriander powder and chilli powder and mix well. Add the tomatoes and cook till the oil separates. Stir in the cooked *dals*, salt and more water if required. Cook for ten minutes stirring occasionally.
4. Add the *garam masala* powder and serve hot, garnished with coriander leaves.

PUNJABI KADHI

My absolutely favourite comfort food.
I love coming home to kadhi chawal after a trip abroad... because I miss it so.

Ingredients

Pakore

¾ cup gram flour (*besan*)

1 medium onion, chopped

½ cup chopped fresh fenugreek leaves (*methi*)

1 inch ginger, grated

1 teaspoon carom seeds (*ajwain*)

1 teaspoon red chilli powder

¼ teaspoon baking powder

Salt to taste

Oil for deep-frying

Kadhi

1 cup yogurt

¼ cup gram flour (*besan*)

1 teaspoon turmeric powder

Salt to taste

2 tablespoons oil

½ teaspoon fenugreek seeds (*methi dana*)

½ teaspoon cumin seeds

6 black peppercorns

2 dried red chillies, broken into large bits

1 medium onion, chopped, (optional)

½ inch ginger, chopped

1 teaspoon red chilli powder

Method

1. Mix together all the ingredients for the *pakore*, except the oil, adding about half a cup of water.
2. Heat the oil in a *kadai*; drop small portions of the *besan* mixture into the hot oil and deep-fry till golden brown. Drain on absorbent paper and set aside.
3. For the *kadhi*, whisk the yogurt and *besan* together till smooth. Stir in the turmeric powder, salt and three cups of water.
4. Heat the oil in a *kadai*; add the fenugreek seeds, cumin seeds, peppercorns and red chillies. Stir-fry for half a minute. Add the onion and ginger and stir-fry for one minute. Stir in the yogurt mixture and bring to a boil; lower the heat and simmer for about fifteen minutes, stirring occasionally.
5. Add the chilli powder and fried *pakore* and continue to simmer for four or five minutes.
6. Serve hot with steamed rice.

DAL MAKHNI

Dal Makhni or maa ki daal is a celebrated Punjabi delicacy, or I should say – a Punjabi celebrity! It is loaded with protein and calcium and no wonder it is a beloved winter food.

Ingredients

½ cup whole black gram (*sabut urad*), soaked

2 tablespoons red kidney beans (*rajma*), soaked

Salt to taste

1 teaspoon red chilli powder

2 inches ginger, chopped

1 tablespoon oil

3 tablespoons butter

1 teaspoon cumin seeds

1 large onion, chopped

6 garlic cloves, chopped

2 medium tomatoes, chopped

1 teaspoon *garam masala* powder

½ cup fresh cream (*malai*)

Method

1. Cook the soaked black gram and *rajma* in three cups of water with salt, chilli powder and half the ginger till soft.
2. Heat the oil and butter in a thick-bottomed pan. Add the cumin seeds; when the seeds change colour, add the onion and sauté till golden brown.
3. Add the remaining ginger, garlic and tomatoes. Sauté till the tomatoes are pulpy and the fat begins to separate. Add the cooked black gram and *rajma*.
4. Add half a cup of water and *garam masala* powder; bring to a boil, lower heat and simmer for fifteen minutes. Stir in the fresh cream and simmer for another five minutes.
5. Serve hot with *naan* or *parantha*.

MATAR AUR MANGODI KADHI

I think this recipe is a saviour on a rainy day!
Use peas from your freezer and mangodi from your kitchen cupboard.
In fact, convert this kadhi into a main dish when vegetables are not available.

Ingredients

½ cup shelled green peas (*matar*)

½ cup *moong mangodi*

1½ cups sour yogurt

3 tablespoons gram flour (*besan*)

4 tablespoons oil

½ teaspoon fenugreek seeds (*methi dana*)

½ teaspoon mustard seeds

1 teaspoon cumin seeds

6–8 curry leaves

4 dried red button chillies (*bor mirchi*)

5 garlic cloves, chopped

A pinch of asafoetida (*hing*)

1 teaspoon red chilli powder

½ teaspoon turmeric powder

½ teaspoon sugar

Salt to taste

Method

1. Whisk the yogurt and *besan* well. Add three cups of water and mix.
2. Heat the oil in a *kadai* and fry the *mangodi* till light brown. Remove and drain on absorbent paper.
3. To the same oil, add the fenugreek seeds, mustard seeds, cumin seeds, curry leaves, *bor mirchi* and garlic and sauté for one minute. Add the asafoetida, green peas, fried *mangodi*, chilli powder and turmeric powder and sauté for half a minute. Add one-fourth cup of water and cook over a low heat for two minutes.
4. Stir in the yogurt mixture, sugar and salt. Bring the mixture to a boil, lower heat and simmer for ten minutes till thick.
5. Serve hot.

SOOKHI DAL AMRITSARI

Punjabi cooking calls for a lot of ginger and onion and this dal is particularly heavy on the ginger essentially because urad dal can cause flatulence. I suggest you make this dal and serve it hot immediately with rotis.

Ingredients

1 cup split black gram (*dhuli urad dal*), soaked

Salt to taste

½ teaspoon turmeric powder

3 one-inch pieces ginger, cut into thin strips

4 tablespoons oil

A pinch of asafoetida (*hing*)

1½ teaspoons cumin seeds

2 medium onions, chopped

4–5 green chillies, chopped

3 medium tomatoes, chopped

1 teaspoon red chilli powder

¾ teaspoon *garam masala* powder

2 tablespoons chopped fresh coriander leaves

4 teaspoons lemon juice

Method

1. Place the *dal*, three cups of water, salt, turmeric powder and half the ginger in a deep pan. Bring the mixture to a boil over a high heat, lower heat and cook till just done.
2. In a separate pan, heat the oil. Add the asafoetida, cumin seeds and onions and sauté till the onions are lightly browned. Add the remaining ginger, green chillies and tomatoes and sauté for a few minutes. Add the chilli powder and sauté till the oil separates.
3. Strain the *dal* and add to the *masala*. Mix well and stir in the salt, *garam masala* powder, coriander leaves and lemon juice. Cook for two more minutes and serve hot.

DAL PANCHRATAN

Ghar ka khana or comfort food should have this nutritious mix of five dals on the list. Especially when it's raining and there is no way you can go out to buy vegetables.
Just have bowls of this dal (rice and roti are not necessary!).

Ingredients

2 tablespoons whole red lentils (*sabut masoor*)

2 tablespoons whole black gram (*sabut urad*)

2 tablespoons whole green gram (*sabut moong*)

2 tablespoons split Bengal gram (*chana dal*)

2 tablespoons split pigeon peas (*toovar/arhar dal*)

1 ½ tablespoons pure *ghee*

2 green cardamoms, crushed

1 inch cinnamon

¾ teaspoon caraway seeds (*shahi jeera*)

2 small onions, chopped

1 small tomato, chopped

¾ teaspoon coriander powder

⅓ teaspoon roasted cumin powder

¼ teaspoon turmeric powder

¾ teaspoon fennel (*saunf*) powder

1 ½ teaspoons red chilli powder

⅓ cup yogurt, whisked

Salt to taste

1 ½ tablespoons cream (*malai*), whipped

Method

1. Soak all the *dals* in two cups of water for one and a half hours. Drain and set aside.
2. In a pressure cooker, cook all the *dals* with three cups of water till the pressure is released three or four times (three or four whistles).
3. Heat the *ghee* in a pan; add the cardamoms, cinnamon and caraway seeds and sauté till fragrant.
4. Add the onions and sauté till golden brown. Add the tomato, coriander powder, cumin powder, turmeric powder, fennel powder and chilli powder and sauté for two or three minutes.
5. Add the yogurt and cook for another two minutes.
6. Add the cooked *dals*, two-third cup of water and salt and bring the mixture to a boil. Remove from heat and serve hot, garnished with cream.

Books by Master Chef Sanjeev Kapoor

Small Format

Title	MRP ₹
The Party Food Cookbook	110
Non-Vegetarian Soups and Salads	99
Best of Paneer: A collection of Vegetarian Recipes	99
Cocktail Snacks	99
Desi Murgh	99
Curries	99
South Indian Snacks	99
Roti-Paranthe	110
Vegetarian Breakfast Bonanza	125
Scrumptious Vegetarian Salads	99
Delicious Vegetarian Soups	99
Vegetarian After-School Snacks	125
Vegetarian Soups	125
Recipes for Non-Stick Cookware	125
Vegetarian Cooking with Dahi	110
Go Green	99
Healthy Tasty Recipes	99
Monsoon Medley	99
Chill Out! Summer Eats and Treats	99
Mango Masti	99
Tawa-Handi Recipes	125
Sunday Specials	125
Simple Home Baking	110
Chai-Nashta	125
Mirch Mazaa	125
Sweet Temptations	110
Dal-Roti	99
Desi Sabziyan	110
Pickles, Chutneys 'n' More	110
Say Cheese!	99
Mushroom Mania	99
Noodles and Pasta	110
Makai Magic	99
Eggs	99
Desi Aloo	99
Dahi	125
Rice, Biryani and Pulao	125
Vegetarian Rice, Biryani and Pulao	125
Kadai Cooking	110
Pressure Cooking	99
No-Oil Recipes	99
No-Oil Vegetarian Recipes	110
Street Food	125
Desi Mutton	95
Thai Cooking	99
Paneer	110
Italian Cooking	99
Drinks and Mocktails	125
Vegetarian Breakfasts	125
Salads	125
Non-Vegetarian Recipes from Around the World	99
Vegetarian Recipes from Around the World	110
Seafood	125
Chicken Recipes	125
Punjabi	99
Chinese Non-Vegetarian Cooking	110
Chinese Vegetarian Cooking	99
Microwave Desi Cooking	110
Sweet Encounters	99
Soups, Salads and Sandwiches	110
Vegetarian Snacks and Starters	110
Non-Vegetarian Snacks and Starters	110

Big Format

Title	MRP ₹
The Yellow Chilli Cookbook	595
Mithai - Sweets for Every Celebration	295
Kitchen Library Eat Lite - Low-Calorie Vegetarian Collection (set of 5 volumes)	485
Cooking with Love - Vegetarian Recipes from My Mother's Kitchen	295
Healthy Indian Cooking for Diabetes	345
100 Favourite Hand-Picked Recipes	595
Fun Food for Fussy Kids	350
Kitchen Library Vegetarian Collection (set of 5 volumes)	485
Simply Stylish - Entertaining at Home	395
Wedding Collection - Recipes for Newly-Weds	1200
Dakshin Delights	295
Everyday Indian with Olive Oil	495
Marwari Vegetarian Cooking	295
Tandoori Cooking @ Home	275
Flavours of the Orient	250
Wrap 'N' Roll	350
Party Cooking	295
Dal and Kadhi	350
Chaat	350
T.V. Dinner	350
Cakes and Bakes	295
No-Oil Vegetarian Cooking	275
No-Oil Cooking	295
Konkan Cookbook	275
Simply Indian	275
Royal Hyderabadi Cooking	350
Best of Chinese Cooking	275
Microwave Cooking Made Easy	295
Khazana of Healthy Tasty Recipes	250
Any Time Temptations	295
Low Calorie Vegetarian Cookbook	295
Khana Khazana: Celebration of Indian Cookery	295
Khazana of Indian Vegetarian Recipes	275
Khazana of Indian Recipes	295

NEW RELEASES

Big Format

Title	MRP ₹
Everyday Cooking	295
Aah! Chocolate	595
Low-Salt Cookbook	195
Tiffins - Delicious and Healthy Khana for Dabba	295

Small Format

Title	MRP ₹
Iron-Rich Recipes	110
Vegetarian Finger Foods	110
Kabab Lajawab!	99
Vegetarian Recipes from Marwar	99
Noodles and Rice	99

Buy online from www.sanjeevkapoor.com